Head Louse

**Karen Hartley,
Chris Macro
and Philip Taylor**

Heinemann
LIBRARY

For more information about Heinemann Library books, or to order, please telephone +44 (0)1865 888066, or send a fax to +44 (0)1865 314091. You can visit our web site at www.heinemann.co.uk

First published in Great Britain by Heinemann Library,
Halley Court, Jordan Hill, Oxford OX2 8EJ
a division of Reed Educational and Professional Publishing Ltd.
Heinemann is a registered trademark of Reed Educational & Professional Publishing Ltd.

OXFORD MELBOURNE AUCKLAND
JOHANNESBURG BLANTYRE GABORONE
IBADAN PORTSMOUTH (NH) USA CHICAGO

Designed by Ron Kamen
Illustrated by Alan Fraser at Pennant Illustrations
Originated by Ambassador Litho Ltd.
Printed in China by South China Printing Co. Ltd.
04 03 02 01 00
10 9 8 7 6 5 4 3 2 1

ISBN 0 431 01707 7

British Library Cataloguing in Publication Data

Hartley, Karen
  Head louse. – (Bug books)
  1. Pediculus – Juvenile literature
  I. Title II. Macro, Chris III. Taylor, Philip
  595.7'56

Acknowledgements

The Publishers would like to thank the following for permission to reproduce photographs:

Ardea London: John Mason p.9; Bubbles: Ian West p.17, James Lamb p.28, Jennie Woodcock p.24, p.27; Nature Photographers: Nicholas Phelps Brown p.23, NHPA: GI Bernard p.4, Stephen Dalton p.6, p.25; Oxford Scientific Films: Alastair MacEwen p.15, JAL Cooke p.13, p.21, p.22, London Scientific Films p.11, Science Gallery p.5, Scott Camazine p.12; Premaphotos Wildlife: Ken Preston-Mafham p.14; Science Photo Library: Andrew Syred p.7, Bsip Vem p.20, Dr Chris Hale p.10, Dr P Marazzi p.8, Eye of Science p.26, M. Clarke p.16; Sinclair Stammers p.29; Tony Stone: Caroline Wood p.19, Charles Thatcher p.18.

Cover photograph reproduced with permission of JAL Cooke/Oxford Scientific Films.

Every effort has been made to contact copyright holders of any material reproduced in this book. Any omissions will be rectified in subsequent printings if notice is given to the Publisher.

Contents

Any words appearing in the text in bold, **like this**, are explained in the Glossary.

What are head lice?

Head lice are **insects**. They live in people's hair. When they move about and feed they make your head feel itchy.

All lice are **parasites**. Different types live on other animals in the fur or hair. Some suck and others bite. The human head louse is a sucking louse.

What do head lice look like?

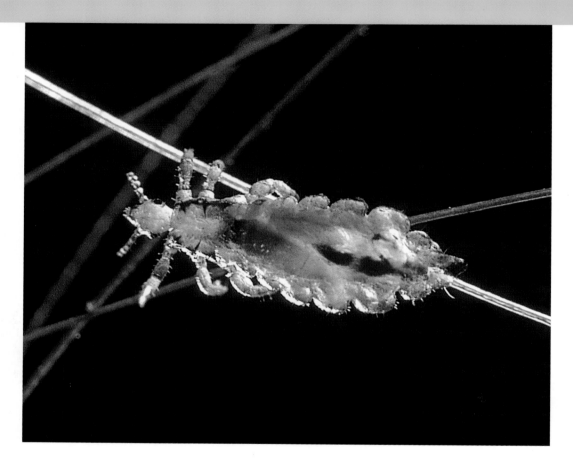

Head lice do not have wings. They have short **feelers**. The body is soft and flat. Sometimes head lice are white and sometimes they are brown.

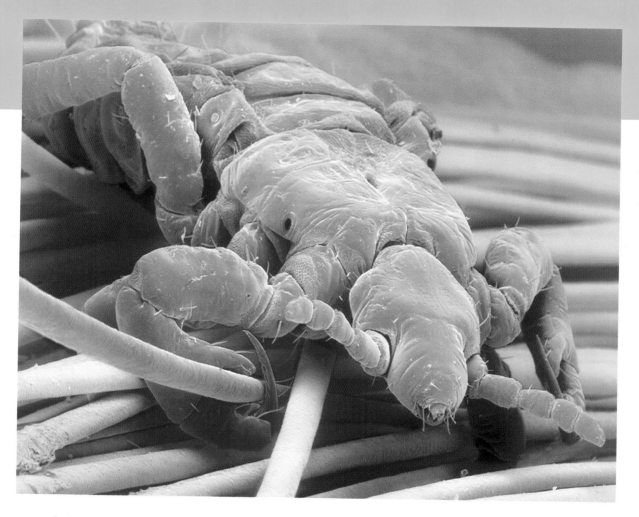

Head lice have short legs with hooks which help them to hold onto hairs on our heads. They have sharp mouthparts called **stylets** which they stick into people's heads.

How big are head lice?

Head lice are very hard to see because they are very tiny. They are about as big as the head of a pin. **Female** head lice are bigger than **male** head lice.

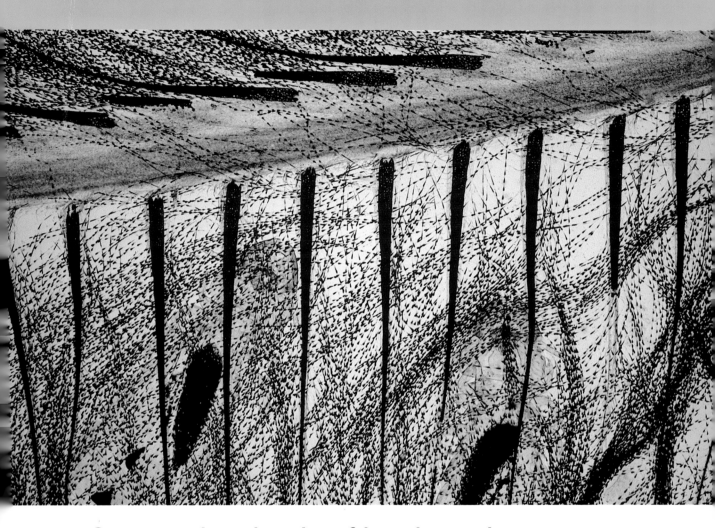

Some other kinds of lice have bigger heads and smaller bodies than human head lice. Biting lice live on birds and eat bits of skin and feather. They do not suck blood for food.

How are head lice born?

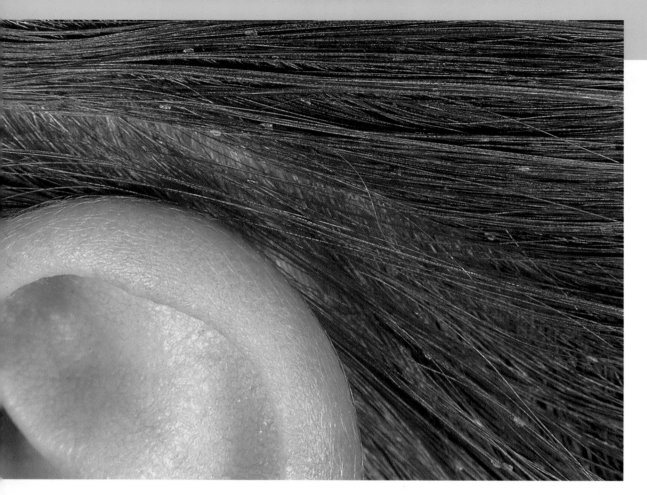

Adult head lice lay about ten eggs a day. They make a glue to stick each egg to a hair. Sometimes eggs are laid one by one but they can be in groups.

When the baby inside the egg is ready to **hatch**, it sucks in air. Blowing the air out helps to push it from the egg. The empty eggshells are called **nits**.

How do head lice grow?

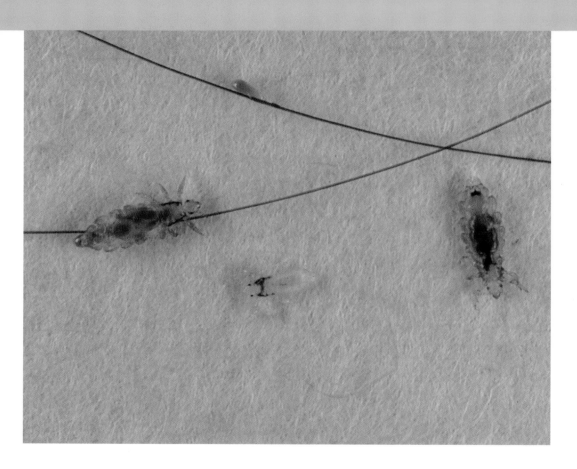

Baby head lice are called **nymphs**. The nymphs are **transparent**. They change colour as they grow to match the colour of the hair they live on.

When the nymph grows too big for its skin the skin drops off and there is a new, bigger skin underneath. This is called **moulting**. After it has moulted three times it is an **adult**.

What do head lice eat?

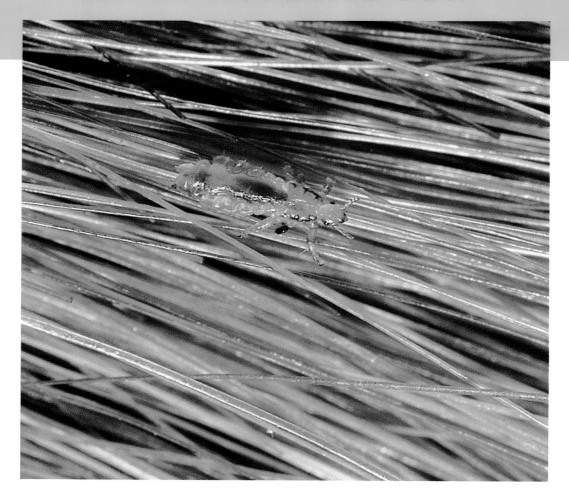

Human head lice only eat blood which they suck from a person's head. They need to feed every five hours so they will have four or five meals a day.

When the head lice are ready to eat they make a hole in the skin with the **stylets**. Then they suck the blood through these special tubes.

How do you attack lice?

People feel dirty if they have lice in their hair. Anyone can catch them, and many people do. When you comb your hair, you can look for the tiny white **nits**.

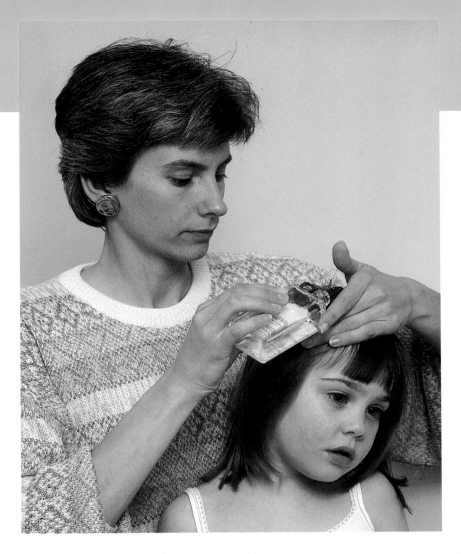

Killing the lice is the only way to become clean. The lice are killed using a special lotion. The chemicals in the lotion kill the lice, so no more eggs are laid.

Where do head lice live?

Most head lice spend all their lives on the head of the same person. Head lice live in the hair of people from all countries. Head lice live on **adults** as well as children.

If head lice leave the person they will die. They need our blood for food and they need the warmth of our heads.

How do head lice move?

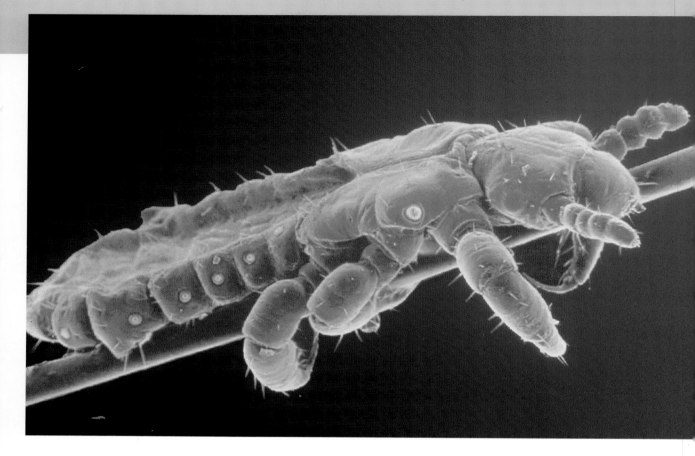

Head lice have three pairs of legs on the front parts of their bodies. They crawl along the hair when one person's head touches another. This is how they are passed on.

Some people think that head lice jump from one person's head to another one. Scientists now say that head lice do not jump!

How long do head lice live?

The whole of the life of a head louse is only three or four weeks long. In this time it can grow big, it can **mate**, and the **female** can lay all her eggs.

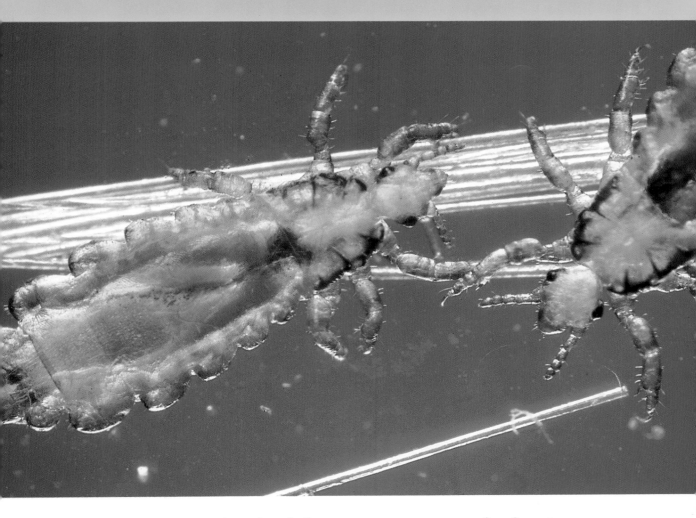

Living its whole life in someone's hair means that a head louse stays at the same **temperature**. If the head louse becomes hotter or colder it will die even sooner.

What do head lice do?

Head lice can tell when another person's head is very close. If people have head lice in their hair you can sometimes see tiny black **droppings** on their collars.

Some people think that only people with dirty hair have head lice. This is not true. Head lice like clean hair because they can cling on more easily.

How are head lice special?

Although head lice have two eyes, one on each side of the head, they cannot see very well. They can only tell when it is light or dark.

Head lice squirt a special liquid into our heads so we cannot feel them sucking our blood. This liquid makes the **wound** itch afterwards.

Thinking about head lice

Think about what you know about head lice. Can you think why people with long hair might tie it back before they go out?

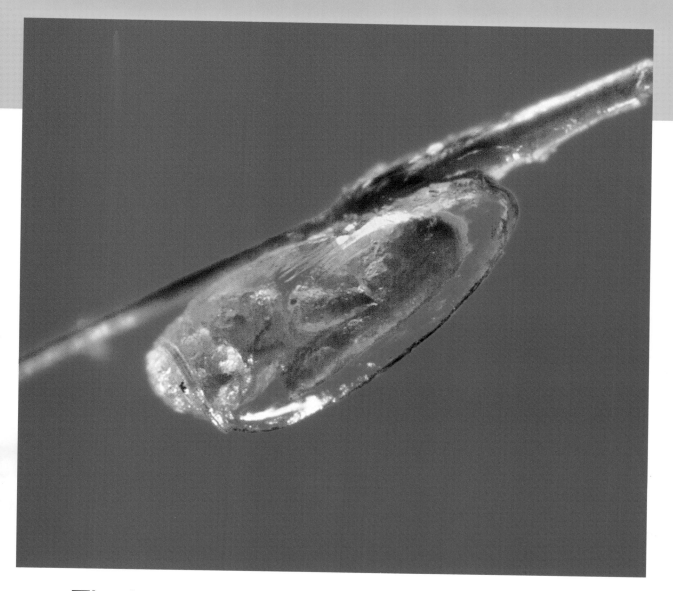

Think about the picture on this page.
Do you know if it is a picture of an egg,
a **nymph** or an **adult** head louse?

Bug map

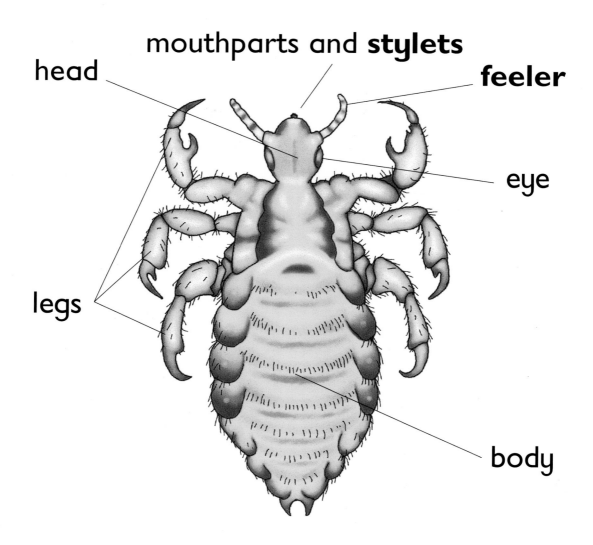

head

mouthparts and **stylets**

feeler

eye

legs

body

Glossary

adult a grown-up

dropping the body waste from an animal

feelers two long thin tubes which stick out from the head of an insect which help the insect to know what is around it

female a girl

hatch to come out of the egg

insect a small animal with six legs

male a boy

mate when a male and female come together to make babies

moult when a head louse grows too big for its skin it grows a new one and wriggles out of the old one

nits the empty egg shells

nymphs the baby head lice

parasite an animal which lives on another animal

stylets thin, sharp tubes which make a hole in the skin

temperature how hot something is

transparent you can see through it

wound a sore place on the body

31

Index